One Thousand Sheets of Rice Paper

Praise for Kevin Cantwell

on *Something Black in the Green Part of Your Eye* (2002):

"Song of the Black Corona," "Choral Lines from the Sumerian," the title poem, "The Wooden Trap"—these poems say that the world is on fire but only the steadiest and most masterful hand can show us the burning. Kevin Cantwell's steady and masterful poems blend poise and intimacy in a style that is his own and built for the ages.

—Frank Bidart, winner of the Pulitzer Prize for Poetry

on *One of those Russian Novels* (2009):

Poems on the deaths of artists and friends, even when they're very long gone, indeed—see "Marlowe in Italy"—hail their subjects' follies and vices equally with their achievements. This is poetry teeming with light, darkness, color, movement, heat, cold, sound, and silence. Reading it is like watching a complicated, demanding movie or, in full consciousness, life.

—*Booklist,* starred review

Poetry by Kevin Cantwell

Something Black in the Green Part of Your Eye

One of Those Russian Novels

Writing on Napkins at the Sunshine Club:
An Anthology of Poets Writing in Macon (editor)

One Thousand Sheets of Rice Paper

POEMS

Kevin Cantwell

MERCER UNIVERSITY PRESS
Macon, Georgia
2023

MUP/ P633

Published by Mercer University Press
1501 Mercer University Drive
Macon, Georgia 31207

27 26 25 24 23   5 4 3 2 1

From "The Return of the Proconsul," from THE COLLECTED POEMS: 1956-1998, Zbigniew Herbert. Translated and edited by Alissa Valles. Copyright © 2007 The Estate of Zbigniew Herbert. Translation copyright © 2007 HarperCollins Publishers LLC. With additional translations by Czeslaw Milosz and Peter Dale Scott. Used by permission of HarperCollins Publishers. "Hitch Haiku," by Gary Snyder, from THE BACK COUNTRY, copyright © 1968 by Gary Snyder. Reprinted by permission of New Directions Publishing Corp. Excerpt from A DIFFERENT PERSON: A MEMOIR by James Merrill, copyright © 1993 by James Merrill. Used by permission of Alfred A Knopf, an imprint of the Knopf Doubleday Publishing Group, a division of Penguin Random House LLC. All rights reserved. From "It Is True All Legends Once Were Rumors," from PALE COLORS IN A TALL FIELD, by Carl Phillips. Copyright © 2020. Used by Permission of Farrar, Straus and Giroux. From THE ODYSSEY. Translation copyright © 1998 Robert Fitzgerald. Used by Permission of Farrar, Straus and Giroux.
Printed and bound in the United States.
This book is set in Adobe Garamond
Cover/jacket design by Burt&Burt.

Library of Congress Cataloging-in-Publication Data
Cantwell, Kevin, author.
One thousand sheets of rice paper : poems / Kevin Cantwell.
1000 sheets of rice paper
Macon, Georgia : Mercer University Press, 2023. |
LCCN 2022045203 | ISBN 9780881468755 (paperback) (acid-free   paper)
LCGFT: Poetry.
LCC PS3603.A63 O55 2023 | DDC 811/.6--dc23/eng/20221212
LC record available at https://lccn.loc.gov/2022045203

for Tamar

CONTENTS

MERCER UNIVERSITY PRESS

Endowed by

TOM WATSON BROWN
and
THE WATSON-BROWN FOUNDATION, INC.

We mapped our way north by the stars, old school, until there
were no stars, just the weather of childhood, where it's snowing forever.

—Pale Colors in a Tall Field, *Carl Phillips*

Instructions to the Coast
Capps, Florida

The St. Marks, the Sopchoppy,
and these that remain unmarked
    waters, black tidal sloughs
you will have to cross at night—.
    Turn left at the liquor store
they have made a church. That's south.
    A white cross, painted thick
on the window, will lean, fall
    across the road when the lights
are on, though that place is shut.
    Had you gone past your turn,
you would have found Sumatra
    soon, then Hosford—Bible towns
no more than coal and timber yards
    lit at night by the helpless gaze
of one train so slow it trembles
    in the dark. Soon, you will want signs.
Turn left when this road ends. That
    is west—but if it is night, and you
have come far, it will seem like south
    again, the constellations wrong.
Drive on—though the dashboard
    compass cocks a flounder's eye,
and this spur becomes crushed shell
    stopped short of the river,
deep sand where many have wept,
    argued with the stars, yet circled
to find another place to cross.

I.

The Problem of Cremation at East Point, Florida

For this kind of fun, they cheat the gulls of bread,
and throw bits of shell, by which they are called back down.
    This trick gets them one short laugh of the day.
They are so broke too they do not have one more thing left
    to touch but their own cold hands
shoved in their pants, and the seams that are sewn folds
    like the tops of seed bags, though not one black seed
clings to the duff of that lint.

The gulls know it is not bread, yet they are so poor
they peck at it while it falls. And then these two men
    try once more to show how lean
a week can get with no check, or how the wind will push
    the gray sea to them, and how the gulls
will veer hard, cut through the wind, and if it is
    that time of day, the gray, tin, near side of their wings
will flash as they rise back up.

And if this hour looks like the end,
they have come, from up at the house, where it's been hard
    all day, where they have called their friends
who will not hang up, folks they have owed
    cash from day one, or a car ride or junk for when
those things scratched their need. Now they must
    have more to put their old mom to her last bit of ash,
plus the bill for the gas touched to a white blaze

—and more for at least a waxed box,
or a blue jar, which they have no place to keep or set,
    the house not hers, but just for these
last months, for her mail, a straight chair in the yard,
    the grass not cut, one path to the pale car, one to the sea,

where her two sons fool a bird and make its slow kin
     turn in the high wind, where one more time they must drop down
in the awful tongues of the Pentecost.

This Golden Thread

*[H]ow long, with what desire, I waited! / till, at the twilight hour,
when one who hears / and judges pleas in the market place all
day / between contentious men, goes home to supper, / the long
poles at last reared from the sea.*
                    —The Odyssey, XII

In Dublin city and at Trinity especially
you are warned not to lounge on these green lawns.
        And if in case you are an American,
you are reminded, as well, when lost and driving,
        to keep to the *effing* left. Roundabouts
can be sticky, and if in a Citroen 3 with a boggy clutch
        somewhat more iffy. Yet if you go
round and around, and if you let those who are cousins
        twice removed yield to you, you can
give them the finger twice more around until they
        have had enough of this wit.

        Thus you can be released, from any spell
let go, even that dread pull a swimmer is unfolded from,
        which holds him below so long it is,
as written, a magistrate's day early begun and ended late
        that keeps him in the vortex of that glass.
And if you were one of those drowned U-boat sailors
        now under one stone marker inland
in these barrowed Wicklows, the slant ocean,
        like this pitched land, might let you rise up to see
nothing but two cold ponies chasing crows
        from fence post to fence post;

        or that wrecked Fiat we passed,
teetering on the lip of the right-of-way, burned

    beetle-green then rust and now this
friable husk, its doors exfoliated and puffed ajar
    like a blue locust in the palm
of a Trinity boy—who pulls a leash, a golden thread
    unwound from a tatty hem in the sacristy,
blessed therefore but filched while the priest smoked after Mass,
    its shimmering length needled through
the thorax to demonstrate how, unspooled, its motor
    will make slow turns above them.

Old Miami

Levine used to say if you remember one of his readings
that Donald Justice had never seen

a worker, and Justice who had practiced his childhood piano
on one of Miami's old streets

could recall a sunburned man with a bucket of masonry trowels
who had walked by the porch window of his piano teacher

one summer at the end of a lesson hour, his red hair
stiffened by mortar.

The Night Merle Haggard Could Not Go On
Macon, Georgia, January 17, 2012

Pine fires burned the last gift-wood at the New Year,
and chimney smoke drifted down the bungalow streets.

A few floors up in his hospital room, he grew chilled,
not even a nurse down the hall after dinner.

His face the color of ice on the road, he closed his eyes,
listening to it snow outside, and those grains of sleet

fell through him, like a grip of sand down a well.

From That Shithole Country

we who have ditched your roads for a thousand years
who have swept your streets
fell in a gust at Fredericksburg
who comforted your children
who gave you the plaint you know
as your mountain twang
who tended your parents through the injury
of their old age
or were those clerks of the law
who kept you from prison
and brought you the black Guinness of your evenings
and your rainy weekends
who have taught you that
twist of the mouth
after a secret has been shared
and have taught you
apparently nothing
who have gone over carefully the Irish
for the blackbird's
yellow nib so country we joined the Marine Corps
to get a haircut
so country we take a bus to the Kroger
so country we came over on a boat
our brothers and sisters
a deck below
writhing as ballast
so country we baked
a cornbread wedding cake.

Unrecorded Bird Calls at Night

Florida Panhandle

On the Forgotten Coast of this soon-
to-be forgotten empire, the green
    bottles and our glass jars drop like rain
in fat explosions.

    Boxing recycled glass, we've heard
it twice, though it seemed like
    dreaming from across a lake
startled into daytime words.

    Our tiny voice recorder
picks up ten thousand shrill
    insects but not the burrowing owl
I touch Play to hear.

    From across the road it calls
but will not be recorded here;
    yet now we know, at this hour,
how these woods become unreal.

In Philadelphia

    Hazlitt has seen a hummingbird
like a fives-ball buzz past
      his ear and now these fireflies
sold in a capped cone of paper by a man
      who lights his face by them.

    His father has written ahead
looking for a position, something
      behind the pulpit; anything would do
if he were someone else and not
      this dissenter. No money

    for university, William will paint
Coleridge, trying to drum up
      a life, this portrait Wordsworth will dub
a *horror*, at which—this too is his word—
      one can *sup*. In the morning

    woodpeckers rattling
that new sound and a slave
      below the window having some words
with himself while touching a bag of dust
      at his throat

    —but let us come back to this
portrait, long after the day:
      It made C. look disturbed, touched
in some way, and so he was kept
      faced to the wall if there were visitors.

Hard, Red Box

The thing that gets me most about Huckleberry Finn,
besides the way he mumbles, *Yes, m'am*,
when the widow will ask him if he loves Jesus
as much as Jesus loves him, besides
those good manners, or the way he will mop
butterbean juice from his plate
with a biscuit, or how he can hold his own
against those itchy tricks of her theology—
this: he will slip outside into the dusk
after supper, and though these spiders will touch
his face in dream, he will reach around beneath the porch steps
for his Marlboros, a hard box as he insists upon
at the convenience store by the River,
though that woman too will harden
her lips at his simple ways, his bad habits
known already around town—then, this
is the thing, he will lie down in the stiff grass,
the shadows of his face long in the flare of the lighter,
and then the smoke adrift as his own life
has begun to go away from him, as it had
that day they had tried to raise him from drowning;
and how he was game, some pages later on,
dressed in blue taffeta, threading the squinty eye of a needle;
and how—after Pap had beat and beat him
with a fan-belt, asking him again and again, *Say, say!
Do you want to dress like a* girl—he would try hard
to smile and he would pat down his clothes
for a cigarette, though he could not answer, even in St. Louis,
a town big enough to understand who he had become
in the years that would follow, known to get into a car
with nearly anyone who had some blow.
And on the nights he could not sleep he would

strain to hear, until he could no longer, the sounds of the boats
pushing upriver; and he would tell, until whoever it was
he was with could not listen to more of it, the sun-lit tale
of when they thought he had drowned, persuaded
by superstitions, that a cannon booming over the green,
glass water, would bring him back; and though he knew it
was more of their foolishness, he would ask again
and again (he got like this when he was tired, his head
shaved and a blond wig hooked on the back of a chair) if that meant
they had loved him. *Say*, he would ask, *Say?*

Outside Concord, Massachusetts
Matthew 13:24–30

And there was the day the young Waldo Emerson himself
still did not know what his first sermon would be; the circuit preacher

had written he would not come back to this unruly congregation,
its bug-eyed disputants; so, they had turned to the divinity student, bare arms

scratched from work late on an afternoon, the porcelain chill of evening
now come, hogs to be fed, nothing written down. He confided his worry

to an old neighbor he had cut hay with growing up, who told him
wishing was like a prayer, that the broken chaff was but a cloud unto the sun.

At this, Emerson had glanced upward, and though ashamed the worry
fell from him, like an extra wool shirt dropped in the workday heat,

the itch of that stifling hour, which had seemed unbearable; but days later,
an hour early, he had taken the first steps onto its porch, the cool shade

of the air inside the church house, the cuts on his arms stung
by the starch of his white shirt, and in one coat pocket a clutch of straw—

to be tossed up in demonstration, though, in the end, he did not,
as they had seen for themselves how the red sun trembled as it rose.

Blind Horse

U.S. Grant at Mount McGregor, New York

If he loved the skittering cut of his skates through the snow-whitened swamp
    oaks,
as night came on and a farmer lit a bonfire against the cold,

he loved the Hudson River more from the high bluffs at West Point;

if it were that summer morning in drawing class when he tried the new
    sharpener
from France and smelled the turned graphite and cedar together, it was then

that gradient river, dropped down from the sketched hills, that he loved more;

if he loved the evening frost and the windfall pippins weighing down his coat,
it was how his pony bobbed its head, breaking their skins, that he loved more;

if it were Virginia tobacco and the way a fresh stogie mingled with pine smoke
from a lit splinter he had loved, it was now the laudanum his sergeant prepared
and the ink smell of dead leaves, the pain put off, that minute he loved;

if he loved his horses, he loved their names; if when he was dying, he recalled
his coveted pony: how he paid too much for it and angered his father;

how he came to sell the horse when it went blind; and how he chanced upon it
years later, circling the gear it turned, pulling a canal boat, it was the colt
he remembered, for which he would slip out to the barn at sunrise, it was then

the apple of its breath he loved most, and the sweet hay nipped from his hands.

My Beautiful Black Slippers

This time we have been touched up by the cold hands
of London Heathrow, made to pass through one more security point
mid-route from Newark on this midnight ticket.
Instead of non-stop to Northern Ireland, this might be
the first days of the forever war and this extraordinary
rendition, Shannon Airport itself, our transport without manifest,
our loosened clothes intimate as pajamas, our passports
lifted from our possession.

They have blocked the stairwell ahead and pull down
the mesh of a steel curtain and bolt behind us two glass doors.
We are detained in this underground hallway, in receipt
we might wonder of a black hold pitching on a black sea
and torture by proxy. In queue with the citizens of Gdansk
and Reykjavik, I remember a taped-up box posted from the Republic.
The clerk had cut a square window into which she inserted
her fingers for contraband but touched only sea glass
wrapped in paper and some freckled aggregate stones
polished at the Moy estuary.

Tonight, the fluorescent tube-lights hiss and shudder on.
We are handed back our papers, let forward, waved to one more stop.
Were this a laughing matter I might say I have come here
beltless so as not to hang myself. My beautiful black slippers too
are easy to remove. Their red soles represent, as did the late Pope's
red shoes when he lay in state, the blood of the martyrs…

As for the guard, he is not privy to my quip
though he is hard for my destination. Belfast. He looks over
his glasses. *To what end?* To read a paper at Queens University.

On which theme? The dialectic of the political in Seamus Heaney…
His face softens. *Ah,* he admits. *The author of Beowulf.*
I clutch my effects, step up, my boarding pass clamped in my teeth,
one more reason to keep my mouth shut.

II

The Week Before Christmas

When my wife was finally able to tell our son
we would separate, he told her where I would hide
the deer rifle, a dinged-up Marlin, sold from
the trunk of a car by a house painter. My son
would watch me, after hunting each season ending
at the New Year, oil the receiver and its walnut
stock over a drop cloth, then climb the steep ladder
to the loft where I would lay across the joists
its horse-blanket case, and where, over one more season,
dust would settle upon it, the rifle he had taken
from me, although suicide would not enter our family
again, like a stranger at a block party,
his untoward lowered voice and reeking breath,
that hiss of confession in mixed company, that a deer
pitched down with one shot will sound just like
a bundled square of roofing shingles thrown to the ground at dusk.

That fall, on a weekday before Christmas, I left
the truck empty-handed and walked into the still-dark woods
down a faint road until I saw my brother
tap the brake lights. In the dome glow of his car,
he leant me a cold rifle, unfamiliar, bolt-heavy, the safety
I flicked on and off in starlight before I chambered
a round and changed into the camouflaged coveralls
I had bagged the year before in black plastic with pine straw
and oak leaves to leach the human scent – this, how
were this to go in another direction, I might have been
found months later, leaf-fall scattered upon my body;
though that late night I made my way below
a hill of frozen sedge, delivered from what had touched me
once, like the cold finger of that hitchhiker
I had picked up one night so many years ago,

whose brother lay sleeping in a hospital in the next town,
shot behind his right ear, which this boy would explain
more than once, as if it were complicated, touching
my neck each time from the backseat, this
chill, though he spoke so softly I had to turn my head to hear
how it had been exact and sudden, the way
when something will fall from our hands
we will not wake up.

The Blizzard

Crossing the threshold itself is what makes us forget,
so says the new science of coming and going.
One room or one day to the next, so much
can be set aside. On a school morning, my son slams the door
of the old truck. The next time it is this cold,
he tells me, I should warm up the cab first
before I tap the horn to call him outside.
My own father had ridden a transport into the rain-
blackened woods of the Ardennes. This was outside of St. Vith,
Belgium, and later in life, he repeated from Bonhoeffer:
If you board the wrong train, it is no use
running along the corridor in the other direction.
I was not sure what that meant at first, surprised
that he would say it at all, but believed it to be
about despair, or something like the helplessness of sleep,
as in the early-morning house on holy days of obligation,
he would say from the dark hallway, *Time to go,*
the bus is leaving. And now, after my son is grown,
when driving back from the coast after midnight, his car
has slid sideways into a deer. At home, we switch
the lamp on, then drive nearly to Sardis Church Road
to gather his young family. They pack the baby in our car
and are driven home, and there in the dark
I wait by myself for the amber strobes of the wrecker.
As they had strapped the car seat in, I held the grandson,
and we had hugged each other at how wonderful
the night was, frost sparkling on the high grass,
and freightliners, like Christmas-lit houses,
shuddering past. Sentimentality is a sin.
Shooting a boy in a frozen field who begs for his life
is a sin. One night I walked with my father in the first hours
of a blizzard to buy a snow-shovel from the hardware store,

and as we returned, we had to dip our heads
against the hard nicks of slanting ice.
Years later they would cart him downtown
in the limo-wagon the coroner called a bus.
Neither is this what Bonhoeffer meant exactly,
but going backward will get you nowhere.
And too much sadness is another sin.

Rain

Slides, kicks, loafers, or the sleek Italian slip-ons
so expensive I was ashamed to wear them
        unless light rain speckled their uppers on a short walk
between an evening car and dinner out, but now,
        to pull the garbage to the road, they are yard slippers,
broken galoshes, a slippery figure of speech
        my father was not given to, though he would say,
Frost is on the pumpkin. Or he would flatten
        a newspaper in front of me:
Here is one of your poets: a news item
        about a Los Angeles writer cited for a disturbance
while arguing with his wife about shoes
        for the kids. *That* he could understand.
A couple of times he had asked about
        "Sweeney Among the Nightingales"—
still puzzling him from his classroom days
        after the war at the University of Detroit.
Do not burn down the house. He meant that
        literally. And when I'm climbing his old house ladder,
one of these collapsed shoes takes a fleck of red paint,
        like a nick from a shaving cut or a stray cinder
spotting its alligator hide. From the word *lapse*—
        slip—one thing, then another.

The Lower Savannah River

for Paul Hoinowski

Forgive me. This is not an elegy for the end of snow or those leaves
that redden then fall and fall; and forget the clockwork
   of that broken car a few minutes past five slowing at each house
when those still in pain from surgeries can finally sleep.

The White Top cab moonlights on its paper route.
And those tire chains down the block are now squeaking past in snow,
   but I do not listen for them, nor hear that thump
smack the door, waking me from where insomnia has let me go.

The laptop lights my face. Delivery canceled, no paper
to sheet this table from church shoes polished on a weeknight,
   but there's a tin of oxblood opened neat as red jam.
My old boss called it fish paper if he joked with me on break.

Ours was a survey crew on the lower Savannah River.
Bell's or Henslow's, he knew his sparrow calls; his mud tributaries, too.
   We puzzled the Down and Across by watershed—
and this rippled estuary at dusk, like blackened paper about to burn.

Spring Hawk

The same milk-white underside of its cocked wings
    as this Kilz-primed tongue and groove, sanded

when these ripped boards first smelled like sap turpentine
    a hundred years ago. High, sailing

above these houses, the small hawk head-pivots
    as if hunger has whistled it down.

The toolbox copy of the Peterson guide
    maps these locales as accidentals.

The jet stream has pushed it here, best guess, with rain.
    It disappears up the chimneyed air,

until, chipping paint, I tire of it racing
    its quick shadow-streaks across the yard;

and now these fixes and touch-ups seem feckless,
    though combing primer from the two-inch

with a wire brush unclots the watery white
    from the bristles until it's clean, slick

as the black tail of that Mississippi Kite.

The Peach Trees at Xalapa

Who am I to say that this black gum has one more day
or one more week—easy though it is to punch in the number
    of the tree guy once more, Emanuel X, with his cocked head,
smiling up at me, who has promised, though he and his rig are uninsured,
    he will never be injured? And, yes, it was he who had flirted
in Spanish with my wife, who had, at that exact moment, she will say,
    no more use for him, he does get the job done, he bids low,
and it will come down to him to hitch himself upward then drop it down
    block by block. First each fall to redden in the upper reaches,
this tree has been good to us, broken though it has become,
    poison ivy and thick wisteria emboldened in its kingdom of ants.
Even the peach trees, popping in the fireplace, have risen
    as smoke through the chimney these past two winters, leaving
behind only one cut crooked stick I use after surgery.

I was young when I planted the elbertas, raking small gravel
into squares at the base of each trunk, reading up on how
    they might be pruned, but forgetting about them one year
when our lives seemed to disappear in rain. Then it was the leaf disease
    from drought and a bad mix of poison I had shaken up.
They stood where a cold snap could be drawn downslope by slow water;
    and in a passing vanity, to remind me of Xalapa, I had imagined
that I would use leftover house paint to whitewash the trunks.
    And now I have had so many trees taken down, and after this
shattered gum, there will be the maple, a quick growing trash tree
    lifting the cracked driveway. It must go. Summer after summer
it had shaded my son's room, and leafless in the winter months
    it had let the afternoon sun warm the quilt on his bed
while the old furnace chugged along to do its part.

My son is gone too but only a few blocks away with his family.
Sometimes on his porch with the grandson we will talk
    about how the pecan itself must be pruned back from the eaves

or remember how he and his mom replanted a river birch I had set
    too close to the power line. His mother has gone, and when
that birch no longer crowded the house, we might have wept,
    although the northern windows let in light we had not known
for years until it *whooshed* to the ground. So many trees and brush piles
    burned without permit in Saturday rain. The Sears Poulan
I bought thirty years ago in Salt Lake is hesitant now,
    even if I have placed it in the sun for an hour; the Stihl itself
balks, but it's the new ethanol gas that gives it trouble. Nothing
    is easy we like to say. Even a healthy tree falls for no good reason,
though something inside of it must have been broken.

A Jar of Figs

We are trying to guess its spices,
the small, hand-lettered
jar of preserves open on the counter.

We taste cinnamon and bits of apple—

and standing in the old kitchen
my sweet ex cooked in I can see outside

one tattered mockingbird
stabbing the seeds of a split fig.

Tamar spreads its glop
on a heel of crust—*Delicious,*

she says—*faint clove?*

And that mimic thrush
needling for something else.

Grounds Custodians
Georgia State University, 1979

Our paper routes first but still dark
we walked around the block and stabbed
up trash the wind had blown all night
against chain-linked fences and shrubs

I'd learned to identify then note
on the flattened-out campus map
whose creases became seams of light
tacked by threads when I held it up

to see that it might separate.
That sawed-off broomstick with a nail
sharpened as its tip sometimes kept
the crazies back just out of jail.

We cocked springs of baited rat traps
or with a perfected technique
begrudged as one small mercy
pushed that nail through their necks.

These were the rounds after hard rain
swept shuddering through the city,
this before the cold sun thawed loose
a bung of ice from the valve's T

to let slow water seep through beds
of floribunda cut back for spring.
On frigid nights we threw burlap
on those roses; and snow drifting

through floodlights, we made our way
down the pipe-room steps to crash
on stacked seed bags of winter rye
while the night fell as whitened ash.

Ferlinghetti, North Beach, October 1977

for Katie

I would have been twenty and had hitchhiked with a rain-wet pack from the
    Sierras
to stay with my sister. My climbing ropes were soaked, and the coffee can

that held my Primus stove and its tiny wrenches had rusted over that early fall.
Waiting out the day in a diner, re-counting my money after a plate of fries,

I had seen the bookstore owner by himself. I had the rag of my spiral notebook,
and, sure, I interrupted his quiet lunch, showing him a poem, a page he turned.

He pressed the long fingers of one hand to his mouth. He did not ask me to sit
but said there was that one image, looking up into my face, the old-school
    manners

he made himself begrudge. I sat again at the small table by the corner window.
A few hours later I walked up Columbus Avenue in rain that fell as snow

in the mountains, his owl's face whitened, eyes hooded, as if he looked out,
confused and speechless, from the darkened window of a small apartment.

Santa Maria, 1965

I was too young to know that *corral* comes from the old Latin for *run*.
And it would not have entered my mind to quip that the white horse
snorting over the top rail had used tobacco, although I had seen such
yellow teeth, which my father's father bared, a lifelong smoker himself.

The tub inside the wire fence welled over its rim as the dribbling spigot
kept it stirred, but that morning it was the feeding of the hogs
that scared me, biting each other, eating and shitting, and stepping
on the young. The ranch handyman had shaken stale corn chips

into the long trough from bags unloaded from a Safeway truck.
Then a dairy tanker shot spoiled milk from a black pipe into the mix.
The pigs were wild to be loose and needed only that the iron gate
be unlatched to burst free. Later, I went back to the clear water

of the tank, ignoring a shout to stay back. I knew nothing of a carp,
but submerged nearly the length of the pool this one was blotched,
galvanized too it seemed, drooling black strings of algae, where my own
shadow darkened the water. I got a good look before it fell away.

Ad Altare Dei

In the rooms of Brother X, the lights were never on, except that one black light
on a poster of Dylan made stranger in sunburst than who he was in life;

this was the rectory, quiet, though on a side table a stone fountain pulsed
its welling surface spill and motored through a faint electric hum. Whatever it
    was

I must have said to him that day made him turn on me and hiss a sharp
    warning:
Don't be wise—his spittled badger teeth, whistling and nicotined, less about me

I sensed, than the three of us, not the chosen, together in his rooms, touching
    things
that did not belong to us, objects we did not understand, even a thin wedding
    band—

his mother's. Calm then, he had us try it on, explaining how it would be
    ferruled
around the stem of his chalice once he was ordained. We, too, were there to
    learn

the catechism of the sacraments; and if then we had tested out successfully,
not for the first time, we would be allowed to wear the ribbon of this ornament

on our scout's uniform. *To the altar of God*—I realized a few years later in Latin
    class—
taught not even *that*, instructed in *nothing* to make us believe what would
    remain

unknown to us. And how we would come to forget him, the cold day growing
    dark
on that rainy Saturday; and who of us the first to leave and who of us the last.

The Wooden Flame

for my mother

    A barn plank or a slat from a drift fence to keep the snow
from pouring through: it's made of wood and drawn on it
    a flame, as sketched by a wood-carver's pen, blue, faint
smoke still vapored in the coarse grain. You bought it
    that way from an artist's booth for next-to-nothing.

    You gave it to me to finish up, as if it were that block of oak
I'd carved into a cage that held a ball inside, or that trick
    of whittling that can cut links into a beech-wood chain
from one piece; but I would not take up what someone else
    had begun to make, so you kept it on a shelf these years,
where I would see it, wavering, white from rain, sun-split,
    begun and finished, yet still undone, and drawn on it
a flame.

Sierra Leone

My student Alpha, whose friends have still not returned
from the foothills where one night they hurried

away, says to me
about his fellow student who comes to class
late again, this time eating from a bag of corn chips,

that in his country the young man would have been beaten.

And how we both laughed,
ashamed, until we wept,
the way the suitors of Penelope had laughed,
darkened by the baleful whim of the gods, blood
leaking from their nostrils,
their jaws unhinged—

the way a villager, detained
by neighbors, and bound with fencing wire
to a thorn tree, would weep,
twisting away, as if whipped, gasoline
poured upon him,

and how we would have peeled the bark from a limb
to have made it sting more,
and to have in this way warned him from
his appetites,

to persuade him, as my mother would
promise on a summer morning—
that she could give us something to cry about.

Praise for the Early Riser

for Terry

Ornette Coleman died this morning, which is how by that cosmic wall-
    switch
the house lights flicker. This to a colleague as we walk into the building
    together.

She is not so much a fan of jazz she tells me...

But did she *see* those early evening stars last December?
Or is she not a fan of the galaxy or the rim of night like the lip of a Chinese
    bowl?

And did she not notice how the brown thrasher works
the loneliness of its impatient expertise, flicking aside what it cannot use?

Or is she not one for the birds, not even the mockingbird, disheveled cousin
to the catbird, who regards from the tin rain cap of the chimney
the long hour of summer?

Has she not *seen* the neighborhood fox, sitting at the traffic light, coughing
the way a fox will clear its throat, watching a log truck climb a grade?

Or is she not a fan of these steep hills, which hasten the rain unto the sea?

Does it matter not when Ornette Coleman would carry his loafers in one
    hand,
his saxophone case in another and slip down the wooden stairs?

Or is she not a fan of those who rise early in courtesy of a sleeping
    household?

Has she not heard his first note tested against the fog blast of a tug on the
    East River?
Has she not heard the three chrome snaps of his black case shut one last
    time?

After the Prayer of Saint Francis

i.m. Seaborn Jones

In one night the green leaves have been made to rust.

What we have praised we have not praised enough.
That early morning, before the funeral, the white moon
reddened in eclipse, but only a few of us
rose from sleep to see it burn.

If we have not done all we might have done, begin now
to bless this stranger we once knew.

If what we have meant we have not said again and again,
say this once more, that we have loved this life.

And that glass jar of cold coffee, lift it up
after the microwave has rung its bell and taste
what our dear friend will never have again,
so bitter, so good.

If you will not forgive the friend of your enemy,
begin now to forgive yourself.

I had promised to cut up that pine
pushed down by heavy rains
one night across his yard.
Instead, I shopped for new pajamas and set them
folded on the chair by his front door—

that his broken body might be clothed in linen;

and that, while the bark would loosen
from those branches,
the white sedge, like the candling vapor of heat,
would rise through them,
as our wild angers will flare and collapse,

so that we shall receive,
so that we shall be pardoned.

III

One Thousand Sheets of Rice Paper

If I were Frank O'Hara I would call instead of write
to share this chestnut
firsthand—that when I first met my friend's friend
Ellis Waters, who liked to tell us he had studied painting,
I thought he might enjoy knowing
the Rogier van der Weyden portrait I had just seen
once more at the Met, one I have always admired,
a small oil on wood, standing by itself
so that a Sunday museum crowd would not see it until it had to
walk around its pedestal,

but he dismissed paintings like that—
about things that were *real*,
he said, which made me close my eyes a little
and think he was one more of those idiots.

I am not someone who can hide his emotions
so he must have seen this pass over my face.
He was not angry himself, but still
he waved his hands to show me
how much he loved the black inks of Robert Motherwell.

He would tell me that story of the Dragons and Clouds
rice paper and why Motherwell completed
fewer than six hundred.
He said this leaning forward...

Motherwell had gone to buy origami for a child's birthday
and found this beautiful paper
a master had made,
ten reams each of a hundred,
a sheet the size of this typing paper.

And so this story, one piece at a time
upon which he threw fountain pen ink
from squat bottles, Parker and Sheaffer,
those old names our fathers would have known,
first black, then the dark, nearly petroleum blue
in violent blots, and Motherwell, naked
except for his glasses in the summer heat, sweat dripping,
for weeks, sometimes forty sheets of it in a day,
until his close friend David Smith died
overnight. And that was that,
as it has been now for my friend's friend
Ellis Waters, who has set out from the small village of his life,
and Motherwell, who painted one more time after a stroke,
and of course Rogier van der Weyden
who has descended
these narrow stairs,
the light from above
fainter with each step down,
entering what he would have to become
accustomed to,

this Netherlandish painter who has finished
the small upholsterer's hammer in this young man's hand,
which is, at least, of this
one world we know, real, as some of us who are
so foolish enough to call it
might believe, although his subject is the illegitimate
son who carries in his hardened profile
that shame, of which he is
made and which makes him
quick to anger, though it might be
this winter crowd pressing past him
whose clothes fume with the first minutes of this ashen rain.

The Nostalgia of the Infinite
—de Chirico

The piazza emptied of birds, vast, cold, and the boreal flares
of those high red pennants unburdened of frost;

and the paper cups of carnival thrown down with the leaves;
and that dream she had of a man costumed as a blue crow...

The Black Stone

After a white limo touched its red brakes in fog
then climbed the iron span of a bridge, one side of the molten river
in dusk, the other, night;
after the swifts returned to a crease of shadow;
after the dream of rain…;

                              after I set these lines aside…

I began talking to myself as if to another stranger.

And sometimes, late into an evening class, and long after
my students had huddled on break,
pressing the last streams of cigarette smoke high into the cold night,
the palm of my hand would rise and fall across the desk.

This is how they would come to know that black stone dipping upon the
      surface.

This is how I would demonstrate the accent,
how the poet would hit the syllables—

how a stone skipped hard across a pond glanced upward, and how it fell.

The quicker the line, I would say, the fewer the accents,
the slower the line, more.

How many had come through my class
startled to hear the *thump* of my hand the first of five times?

I was no one either to be remembered,
but over the years, if it were raining on a dark afternoon,
I would call Richard in New York,

who was summoned, he liked to say, when he was young, to Auden's walk-
    up—
and Wystan himself had visited the old maid's flat

Housman kept, his jots of Lucan set out and flies at a windowsill of apples.

This—as far back as that thief
who would take from Christopher Smart's hand,
if he raved in the yard of the asylum,
that folded and unfolded page of lines from the Hebrew of David,
which he had learned would quiet him

if he read them out loud, as though he were merely speaking.

An Essay on Typography

Hopkins would say they *fettled* these flecks of light from alloy
as steel dust—these jewelers who cut letters of type from stock.
  With a bird's-tongue file, they shaved the burrs and nicked
the chaff they puffed aside to make the slant font display
  a book hand meant to imitate Petrarch's script.
They set without kerning one wavering page of *Nature*
  wedged in a proofing tray by wood-block *furniture*
and shimmed *quoins*—but first they waved each glyph
  through candle flame, smoke-pressed it onto wet paper.
One apprentice touched a hot italic to his forearm,
  and his inky boy, so cold, so soon, so this forewarns,
in their rooms above where the town's rank sluice would fall and disappear,
  let his fingernail, in a chipped polish dubbed Purple Seed,
pick the scab to make the letter bleed.

At the River House Bar and Grill

The Wedding-Guest sat on a stone:
He cannot choose but hear...

I

Rain like pea gravel sleets against the window as the storm bells up, rattling the glass in cracked putty—that while her freckled hand, cold with heavy rings, grips my wrist.

The groom, the best man, and the tide-going-out river pouring into the sea: that was her story, fraught as she told it, her hands through her hair, at the dusk-end of a wet afternoon.

At the shadow reaches of the communal table, her friend relishing that same catastrophe, but more slowly:

the beautiful groom, oh, no sailor he, and the best man, then in a new boat, an extravagant gift the day of the wedding, slipping on the tide-shift out to sea; no gasoline to make it back in; no ship-to-shore radio; no water to drink but the endless pewter of the Gulf . . .

Why, she kept asking, *why* not take it *up*river from the marina for a test run? *Why* out to sea?

II

I had seen the news but had not then known her people.

For a week there had been a paragraph in the paper, then nothing, until the next year a small boat was winched from the ocean by a container ship. The best man had strapped himself into three life vests and let the ocean take him up-coast past the phosphorescent wash of sandbars and the lights of night-time cities whereby two days later the full-moon spill carried him in;

but the raving groom himself going out into the late-day's last darkening sun, as this huge, glittering fish, sequined like a cocktail dress, here set down before us, also fades and loses to our appetites parts of itself, the life-flint of its eyes, and flake by flake its flesh pulled clean.

III

Ours was not the feast of the bride's reception, for she had had her weeping, and though she would keep and water the lush philodendra from the funeral, she moved on.

But now, at this gathering, these who cannot let him go count back the weeks and make us see only what that day's occluded bleb of sun has refracted for us;

here, the evening of a reading by a celebrated traveler:

two lovers, who tell this same story, at either end of the planked table: their separation, too—how we know and now guess they have ended it, candles lighted down the table, the magnificent fish, split, spilling its rice-with-capers stuffing;

and her murmuring epithalamium:

IV

the groom, a boy still lean from golf, going out under the roar of
outboards, all the hours of the morning before him, but none slanted to
his favor; and she, his aunt or one-time ex or cousin, one more part of
this I have lost from a story whose strangeness, despite her carrying on,
she had loved to tell;

though finally we have all settled for the quiet of our thoughts;

and, now:

the white stays exposed, ribs of this fish, or umbrella tines of fronds he
might have worked through the Victorian-black cloth of his shirt and
cocked for shade, the couture of shipwreck:

V

not to have chosen otherwise and motored upriver to an inland marina instead and bought a single navel orange and fed her slices before the summer wind-chimes of forks against

the wine glasses of a hundred guests.

Approaches to the Karnaphuli River

Scrap brass/dumpt off the fantail/falling six miles.—Gary Snyder

Our talk, that drift, was maritime.
On the Cold War's rusted oceans,
the Dutchman Raaff had been a swabbie
on a tender—so it was he

I had quizzed about that light line
shot from shore to a ship awash.
A hawser cable, attached to it,
could then be winched across the tide.

We could not recall the gun's name.
The words for gizmos made trouble
for him; yet though his English slipped
sometimes, he'd been an engineer

way back when on the Space Coast
day-dreaming of chipped brass flickering
down through the Mindanao sink.
Retired, Raaff had his project of stairs

circling upward to an outdoor deck,
which was like, gazing through its turns,
the intake of a nautilus valve
glistening as new machinery.

He unfolded a wooden rule
and thumb-marked one-sixteenth
of clearance that makes the miracle
of parts that pass but do not rub.

Later, it did come to me, dark
under the Karnaphuli map
above my kitchen worktable,
it was a Lyle gun, squat and brass.

So, the first line projected slant
as the gun could launch it; the other
then, the next thicker cord, spliced on;
and, once more, an even stouter

hemp drawn to the foundering boat,
until it pitched as a suspension bridge
they'd fashioned to rescue a crew
from drowning; but again, weightless

and buffeted, that first filament
tossed through the dusk, like that sparrow
dipping through the window of light
through this room then into rainstorm.

An Empty Surfboard on a Flat Sea

… reminds me once again that good swimmers drown
    and that the will is vexed so easily.
        I paddled beyond the surf, the ripping sea,
the magnesium horizon far withdrawn,

and, napping, saw three dark fish drop like something thrown
    thus in dream three coins falling through the sea
        (I said the will is vexed so easily.
The ripping sea becalmed. Good swimmers drown.)

and dropped below that spar of glass, the light withdrawn
    through that bubbled dome and could barely see—
        swimming upward yet I fell—the emerald sea
and a starling-cloud of brit unfolding on its run,

which reminded me that good swimmers drown
    and that, like the alchemist of John Aubrey
        who met *the spirits coming up the stairs like bees,*
the will is vexed so easily.

Container Ships on the St. Mary's River

On West Portage in Sault Ste. Marie
you can sit in one of the bars that look north

and count the ore boats riding the dropped water down through the locks,
from Superior to Lake Huron,

a boat like a Potemkin city block lowered on a lift
and winched away by a black rope.

You can watch a barge of coal nudged upstream
into the concrete pen, rising

two decks in fifteen minutes and watch a deckhand step down the ladder
of that rising ship and stay on bubble

with the level eye, like a glass half empty
held up to see the short day it takes the winter sun to slide away.

Even after you leave
the Whitefish taproom, the levered arm of the pour drops and rises

beneath the oil abstract
locals call *Five Crows Nailed to a Barn.*

The Yellow Sun Sawmill

This black sign, though it was faded yellow
when you began to stare, burns
 where this shop has been for years.

 The help has gone. They have left
the grass to its wants and devices, entangled
 to these doors—but this saw

 and its half ton, stone-still,
still spins in crenulated waves that lap its rim.
 In divots of rust yet one note

 long reverberated
when at auction a ball-peen struck it like a cymbal.
 Axled by nothing, it does not turn,

 though boards of pine once shuddered
off the cuts above a pit, glassed by air,
 like one of those globes where human action is

 refracted in another lens.

A Speckled Stone from the Big Two-Hearted River

i.m. Richard Rothman

Years out of law school you had moved on to fishing
the Gulf Stream, the glass rod, thick as a sapling, nearly splintering
    under a marlin, but now these years: the Fenwick fly-rod
you had given me leans in its tube next to an ice axe in the tool room
        dust.
Such lapses too that I have become a Midnight Mass Catholic
and you, from Queens, never less observant. Today, I select
    from this wicker basket one speckled stone, buffed by the ruminant
tonnage of the Laurentide Ice Sheet, until its aggregate
    became this ovoid glass, which our mothers might have kept
for show in a small brass nest on a mantel. I wrap it in paper
    and box it to my sister, your widow, so that she might place it
with her left hand at the unveiling, where it will rest weathered
    still more by those hands that heft and set it down, as I had once
lifted it from that coldest of rivers, pouring into Lake Superior,
    water over stone; and stone upon stone upon stone.

The Ship of Night

I. After Martial

Neither wish death, nor fear his might.
— Henry Howard

My friends, if it is happiness
you want, from what I've learned prop up
    the kitchen window when it rains
so softly you won't hear it stop.

Turn off the news and let your heart-
beats slow to that faint bump we hear
    that once loud bang pulsing from space
through endlessness to reach us here.

And if you have been pricked by slights,
be as Saint Francis says the first
    to text a friend and put out wine,
olives, hard bread that cannot last.

Pick up the strewn yard at first light.
Let your partner sleep. Cut a branch
    of pyracantha for the vase.
The stars are vast; this life, an inch.

II. So Saith the Gospel of St. John

The older and uglier you get, the better your clothes must be.

◆

If a car races up behind you on a rainy highway, let it pass.

◆

A hypocrite is a teenager who has grown up.

◆

If you kick a dog, it will bark.

◆

Do not be the first to arrive at the party.

◆

If they say it's not about the money, it's about the money.

◆

Just because they throw a stick doesn't mean you have to play fetch.

◆

If you must wear pajama bottoms all day, wear a pressed white shirt to
dress it up.

◆

If you must ask for a cigarette, ask a stranger.

◆

Keep a dark suit, a ruby tie, and black polished shoes at the ready.

◆

When driving to work before daylight, a dog will run out to bite the
    tires.

◆

You can turn your life around but not the ship of night.
◆

As for those cabbies of yellow four-door beaters citing Romans in vinyl
        stencils—
    bless them on their first appointments of the day.

◆

A Handful of Dust, not *Brideshead Revisited*.

◆

When driving home at night, a dog will run out to bite the tires.

◆

To those who grip the hand-lettered signs of their extremity, provide
      cash and cold water,
    which shall spill, so saith the Gospel of St. John, everlasting.

◆

If the woman at the table is weeping, set down water, a menu, and come
back later.

◆

A hanging in the morning will clarify the mind.

◆

Do not play cute with the law.

III. Cabin at Sognefjorden, Norway

*My day passes between logic, whistling, going for walks, and being
depressed. I wish to God that I were more intelligent and everything
would finally become clear to me...*
                                                    —Wittgenstein

He was the former president of the college,
and though it was not a stroke something
had happened to him.

Now he unlocks an office after the evening janitors
begin their vacuuming. If it is winter
the campus lake below darkens as the night becomes silver.

He is writing a paper on Freud's last days.
After the lies and all that unhappiness
it was Jung who would look after his needs.

We had both read philosophy,
and when we were much younger
he had invited me to his suite for coffee.
He wanted to impress upon me
that we all have to put aside
a part of who we are to complete the work we are given.

I said I understood.

He himself had climbed the steep, overgrown slope
from that shore to reach Wittgenstein's cabin
where the writer had lived
for a year, and which, in a furious culmination,
had burned in less than an hour.

Tourists on the lake had seen the fire

and not knowing what it was
commented upon it at dinner.

As a way of convincing me that day he had stood on a chair
to take from a shelf charred planks from that fire.

But tonight I look over the lake
and ask myself why it is that Eros will not
integrate and what part of myself I want to forget and why
it is the shimmering water I have come to love.

for Loretta Clayton

IV. Seneca

Late in the city, dusk of a year, when Sun Ra chanted in the uptown
    Amber Room,
we would wait out the invisible
thumping press printing the collected and the acclaimed

or the bitter inks of the new Thucydides.

Apples and popcorn sprinkled with curry and salt—
not much remained after rent.

The marmalade of the binding glues gone brittle,
it's the *Letters* I read;

but today I have spent a January hour splitting broken paperbacks into a
    burn barrel
where a dried Christmas tree

roars like one of the constituents of Nero
wreathed in pitch.

V. Chekhov in Paperback

Soon, but not today, I will leave behind this cotton town, sulfur-blown
from the far-off, smoking mills, its sun-setting dailiness, for the coast; leave,

as it has dropped me, its wire-strung whitened gourds to those itinerants we
           call them now
purple martins or the transmigrating souls of popes.

Someone else must saw back the ginkgo each year and tar its weepy cuts
and learn by heart on which bleak night the yellow leaves will drop at
      once...

My friends ask around what kind of haplessness has come my way

now that editions signed for me can be found on the tables
of used bookstores, even as I have come across,
at Goodwill, a book of my own inscribed to a friend.

He must have boxed up the life he had hoped to know when he retired.

To him my quick theme had been enduring thanks
and, as one will do, I had slashed through my typeset name.

Was that my everlasting shame or was that a taste of pride?

And though it has taken me time to find a way to this forgiveness,
I will sometimes wave to him walking the neighborhood, staying fit, older,
      in one of those caps.

And how still this solitary night as I stop a puzzled fly with this rolled-up
      sheaf...

Whoever *thinks* I will read *Sakhalin Island* again,
or remembers that cold exile of the Japanese Archipelago

pounded by the northern ocean,

or where once, down a slick plank, the ailing doctor
had steadied himself onto the surf-blackened treads

upon which even Bashō would have been careful?

Black Mountain

poem beginning with a line from James Merrill

Who in his right mind wants to know what lies ahead?
Not I, unless it is that hour we are to be released from storm where then

the sun burns through and from the wet trees along this slow river
the last of the night's rain is shaken loose. In two short convertibles,

four of us, my ex in Wyn's MG, a car ahead, a scarf behind her snapping
soundlessly like a dusk-reddened flag in the deathless air of de Chirico.

We are driving, through rags of mist, the river road the long back way
to Marlboro College, closed for the summer, shut for good,

yet, for something to do, we have decided to see its clapboard buildings,
around which from tangled brush the whitened faces of snags stare out.

Larry Levis is gone for years, even the talk of convention corridors,
all the weary elegies we've sung salted in the gravel of his ash.

Liam Rector, for our brief visit at least, is still alive, and in his smoky
ragtop, banged-up, black, an MG, too, I think, we ride.

On another day we might have had less patience with mere happiness,
but that week we are on our own off to Montreal to hear the drums

in the upper woods on Mount Royal, or we are coming back,
and if it is the trip I remember, we will pay out a few more bridge tolls

into the late city where we will sleep only long enough to rise in
    darkness.
Our friend Penelope bruises with Abraxane, but before the end

I will red eye into Detroit Metro, and we will watch the thick snow fall
one more time outside a Chinese restaurant in Ann Arbor.

On its patio someone has made tracks across the snow, which now,
while waiting for our drinks, for something more to say, begin to fill.

Shahid is still with us, and at a party he will get down on one knee
and beg each guest to sing "Achy Breaky Heart" with him;

but before the wine, the deep, *dulce* reds, we will have remembered
Black Mountain, and in one long line its wavering ink-brush horizon.

Parable of the Grand Canyon

I've decided to return to the emperor's court
yes I hope that things will work out somehow
        Zbigniew Herbert, "The Return of the Proconsul"

Even the first minister of this shadow interregnum, who had himself
disappeared, by his thankless pains, thousands of his own citizens,

was not now so willing to unfriend the crown prince—whose lieutenant
of dismemberments had arrived with a willowy saw and that entourage

of two slim silver jets and blackened Expeditions, arriving and then,
more slowly, leaving, this cortege caught on CCTV and now streamed

by the Web in the cold gloom of its frozen upload. The surgeon among us
kept that kind of saw, limber enough, he said, for the hard-to-reach

jaundice of a honey locust. Here, at our coffee klatch, we unworked
the small knots whose untying might undo this world of paradox,

though seed-like and hardened by the grease of many tries some ligatures
were unforgiving. Like many we too have listed our enemies

who—upon our word—would go first, were The Day Itself to come;
and often enough I had encouraged the game we called The Canyon,

which asks: What *if* someone were standing at the lip, someone, just like
that, we could shove, and not lose a night of sleep knowing no one

had seen us, except that startled traveler himself we had so judiciously
directed upon the flagstones of that first treacherous step . . .

We are old fools, as I say, a few of us unchastened bookkeepers
of the Republic; and my friend will make the joke he pretends as preparation

for his class in medical ethics, whose shtick will ask if such sins
are *wrong* and then straighten up for us his glassy smile. O, sure, we will find
      our way

home, unmarked by this poisoned symposium; and there will be those nights
we will sit up suddenly from sleep, but that will be the end of our mercy.

Notes

"This Golden Thread." Epigraph translated by Robert Fitzgerald.

"Old Miami." Philip Levine (1928–2015); Donald Justice (1925–2004).

"The Blizzard." St.Vith, Belgium; critical crossroads during the Battle of the Bulge (1944–1945). Dietrich Bonhoeffer; theologian hanged by the Nazis in final days of World War II and author of *The Cost of Discipleship*.

"Sierra Leone." The African country experienced civil war from 1991–2002.

"After the Prayer of Saint Francis." Seaborn Jones (1942–2014), American poet.

"Instrument Case." Randolph Denard Ornette Coleman (1930–2015), American jazz musician and composer known for the free jazz movement.

"One Thousand Sheets of Rice Paper." Frank O'Hara (1926–1966); American poet and art critic; Rogier van der Weyden (d.1464); Dutch painter; Robert Motherwell (1915–1991); American painter and abstract expressionist; David Smith (1906–1965); American sculptor and abstract expressionist.

"At the River House Bar and Grill." Epigraph from "The Rime of the Ancient Mariner," Samuel Taylor Coleridge.

"The Black Stone." Richard Howard (1929–2022); American poet, translator, and editor.

"An Empty Surfboard on a Flat Sea." For a 50th anniversary publication of *The Paris Review*, George Plimpton asked writers to contribute a poem based on an assigned title, with less than one month to write and submit.

"Black Mountain." Experimental college in North Carolina where significant mid-century painters and poets taught, including Charles Olson, Robert Motherwell, Dorothea Rockburne, Cy Twombly, and Josef Albers. First line, from *A Different Person*, by James Merrill.

ACKNOWLEDGMENTS

The author wishes to extend deep appreciation to the editors of the following publications for printing these poems, many in earlier versions.

Arts & Letters: "One Thousand Sheets of Rice Paper"
Barrow Street: "Parable of the Grand Canyon"
Blackbird: "The Week Before Christmas"
The Bitter Southerner: "The Night Merle Haggard Could Not Go On"
The Chattahoochee Review: "After the Prayer of St. Francis"
Commonweal: "Old Miami"
Five Points: "Instructions to the Coast"; "The Problem of Cremation at
    East Point, Florida"; "This Golden Thread"
The Green Mountains Review: "Container Ships on the St. Mary's River"
Irish Pages: "Unrecorded Bird Calls at Night"; "In Philadelphia"; "The
    Yellow Sun Sawmill"
The Irish Times: "A Jar of Figs" (Poem of the Week)
James Dickey Review: "A Speckled Stone from the Big Two-Hearted
    River"; "From that Shithole Country"
Journal of Florida Studies: "At the River House Bar and Grill"
J Journal: "Sierra Leone"
New South: "Hard, Red Box"
One: "The Black Stone"
The Paris Review: "An Empty Surfboard on a Flat Sea"
Poetry Ireland Review: "An Essay on Typography" (reprinted as Poem of
    the Week on RTÉ, Ireland)
Saint Katherine Review: "The Wooden Flame"
Salmagundi: "My Beautiful Black Slippers"; "The Lower Savannah
    River"
Southern Poetry Review: "The Blizzard"